Language Arts
FOUNDATIONS

D1521016

American Education Publishing™
An imprint of Carson-Dellosa Publishing LLC
Greensboro, North Carolina

American Education Publishing™
An imprint of Carson-Dellosa Publishing LLC
P.O. Box 35665
Greensboro, NC 27425 USA

Printed in the USA • All rights reserved.   ISBN 978-1-62399-083-1

01-060137784

Table Of Contents

Table Of Contents

Introduction

In third grade, your child will begin to take the information he or she has learned so far and put it together into more complicated concepts. At this grade level, your child will also begin to work independently, as opposed to the specific directions he or she received in earlier grades.

Beginning in the third grade, children will become increasingly more abstract thinkers. This school year places a heavy emphasis on past, present, and future as it relates to all subjects.

By the third grade, your child can read with fluency. Now, he or she will move away from "learning to read" and begin "reading to learn," by taking on chapter books and non-fiction texts. With *Language Arts Foundations*, your child will gain a full year of practice with these important skills and will therefore develop greater confidence and understanding.

In third grade, your child will learn:

- to produce simple, compound, and complex sentences. **page 31**
- to explain the function of nouns, pronouns, verbs, adjectives, and adverbs in general and their functions in particular sentences. **pages 34–39**
- to determine the main idea of a text; recount the key details and explain how they support the main idea. **Pages 43–45**
- to ask and answer questions to demonstrate understanding of a text, referring explicitly to the text as the basis for the answers. **pages 66–69**

Use the following hands-on activities to practice language arts skills with your child. These activities encourage creativity and logical thinking. Keep in mind that the process, not the finished product, is what is important!

- When your child finishes a book, create fun ways to share the information in the book with a friend. Some ways to do this might be to write a letter from one character to another, create a comic strip illustrating the events of the book, or write a journal entry one of the characters might write.
- Invite your child to write a different ending or new chapter to a story. If your child can do this in a logical manner, he or she has grasped the plot or ideas presented.
- When you vacation with your child, purchase postcards from the various locations you visit. Let your child write important information about your trip on the postcards. Use a hole punch to make a hole in each postcard and fasten them together for a unique travel memory book.

All About Town

Directions: This map shows the stops a bus makes on its route from North Station to South Station. Write the names of the stops in alphabetical order to figure out what route the bus traveled. Then, trace the bus route.

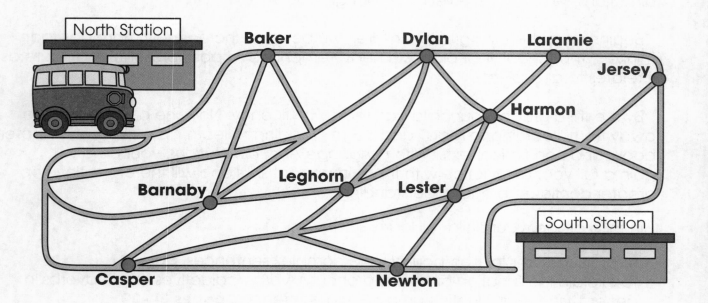

1. _____

2. _____

3. _____

4. _____

5. _____

6. _____

7. _____

8. _____

9. _____

10. _____

Look at a map of your state.
On another sheet of paper, write the names of 20 cities in alphabetical order.

Clowning Around

Directions: Add a word part from the word bank to each blend to make a word that describes something a clown might do in his act.

| _ink | _y | _ow |
| _imb | _asp | _ip |

bl

fl

cl

_____

_____

_____

_____

_____

_____

On another sheet of paper, write a list of action words that start with *bl, cl,* or *fl.*

Twelve Swans Standing Still

Directions: Write the two letters that make up each word's beginning blend. Write **st**, **sw**, or **tw**.

1.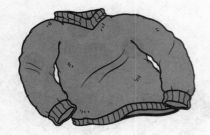

_____

2.

_____

3.

_____

4.

_____

5.

_____

6. 20

_____

On another sheet of paper, write five sentences that include as many words starting with *st*, *sw*, or *tw* as possible. For example: Twins stood on stools in matching sweaters.

Stay on the Path

Directions: Write **ow** or **ou** to correctly complete each word.

1. sc _____ t

2. m _____ ntain

3. tr _____ t

4. fl _____ er

5. sh _____ t

6. sh _____ er

7. t _____ er

8. c _____ nt

Try This!

On another sheet of paper, write a story about a hike in the mountains.
Use as many *ou* and *ow* words as possible.

Say Cheese!

Directions: Write **ch**, **sh**, or **th** to complete each word.

_____umb

_____irt

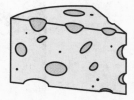

_____eese

_____oe

_____orn

_____eck

_____in

_____ell

_____ermos

Try This!

On another sheet of paper, list five other words for each of the beginning digraphs *ch*, *sh*, and *th*.

Scavenger Hunt

Directions: Part of a scavenger hunt list was torn. Figure out what needs to be found by completing each word with the **ft**, **nt**, or **st** ending.

I. te _____

2. ne _____

3. ra _____

4. a _____

5. pla _____

6. fore _____

7. something so _____

8. footpri _____

Try This!

On another sheet of paper, write four more words with *ft*, *nt*, or *st* blends. Using those words, write a story about a boy who has gone on a scavenger hunt.

Inch Along

Directions: Circle the word that names each picture.

couch   pouch   bush   brush   mouse   mouth

wreath   wrist   bath   bash   ditch   dish

beach   bench   fish   wish   clock   cloth

Try This!

Open a book and find six words that end with *ch*, *sh*, or *th*.
Write the words on another sheet of paper.

Compound Connections

Directions: Cut out the cards below. Combine pairs of cards to form compound words. Glue the cards together on another sheet of paper. Then, draw a picture for each compound word.

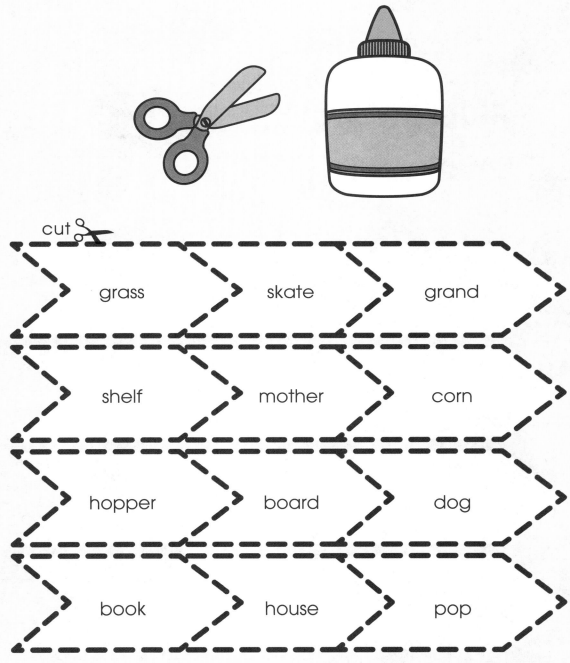

cut

grass	skate	grand
shelf	mother	corn
hopper	board	dog
book	house	pop

Try This!

Syllable Hunt

Directions: Write words to match each clue. Use a dictionary if needed.

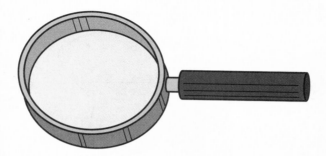

1. Three animal names with two syllables.

_____ _____ _____

2. Two words with four syllables. Divide the words into syllables.

_____ _____

3. Four parts of the body with one syllable.

_____ _____ _____ _____

4. Three names with three syllables. Make sure to capitalize each name.

_____ _____ _____

5. One word with five syllables. Divide the word into syllables.

_____

6. One word with six syllables. Divide the word into syllables.

_____

Try This!

Play a syllable game. Roll a die. Say a word that has the same number of syllables as the number on the die. Score one point for each syllable. The first to reach 20 points wins.

Star-Studded Work

Directions: Write the two words that make up each contraction.

1. aren't _____

2. she'll _____

3. you're _____

4. he's _____

5. you'll _____

6. we're _____

7. they're _____

8. I'm _____

9. can't _____

Try This!

On another sheet of paper, use each contraction above in a sentence.

Buzzing Around

Directions: Cut out the pieces of honeycomb at the bottom of the page. Pair pieces of honeycomb to form new words to match the clues. Glue each pair on the honeycomb.

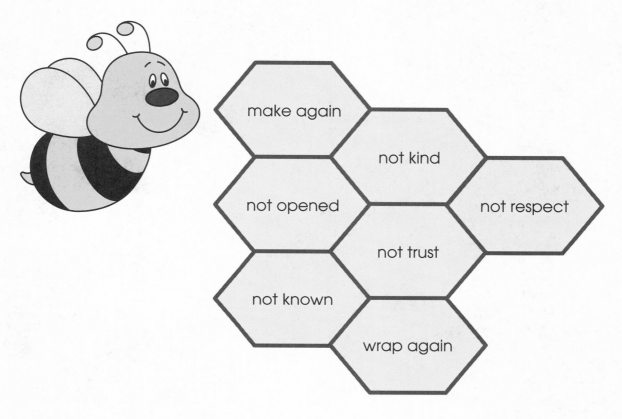

Try This!

On another sheet of paper, use each new word on the honeycomb in a sentence.

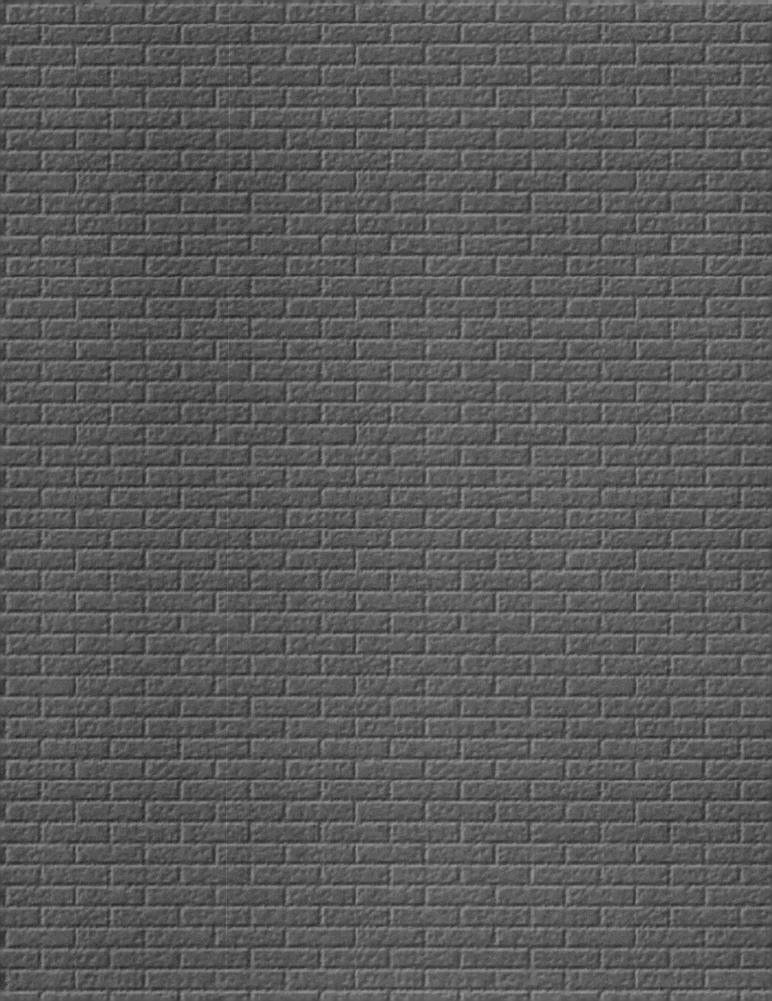

Lizard Tails

Directions: Cut out the cards. Glue the suffix cards to the top of another sheet of paper. Then, glue each card under the correct suffix. Write the new word.

-er

-ful

-less

cut

full of beauty	without color	one who teaches
_____	_____	_____
without meaning	full of doubt	one who works
_____	_____	_____
one who drives	without care	full of thought
_____	_____	_____

Try This!

On another sheet of paper, use each word formed above in a sentence about lizards.

19

The End

Directions: Use the suffixes **-en**, **-ment**, and **-able** to form words to complete the puzzle.

Across

1. something that governs

3. to make harder

4. able to be washed

5. something that is developed

9. something that is shipped

Down

2. able to be read

6. to make lighter

7. able to be enjoyed

8. to make tighter

On another sheet of paper, write 12 other words that have the -able, -en, or -ment suffix. Then, write the meaning of each word.

Synonym Clues

Directions: Write a word from the word bank that has nearly the same meaning as each clue. Use a thesaurus to help you.

academy	bandana	crate
fancy	lurch	nation
rhythm	rickety	section

Across

2. area

5. beat

8. scarf

9. unstable

Down

1. school

3. wobble

4. country

6. box

7. elaborate

Try This!

Find an ad in a newspaper or a magazine.
On another sheet of paper, rewrite the ad using synonyms.

Fishing for Opposites

Directions: Find the pairs of antonyms. Write the words on the lines.

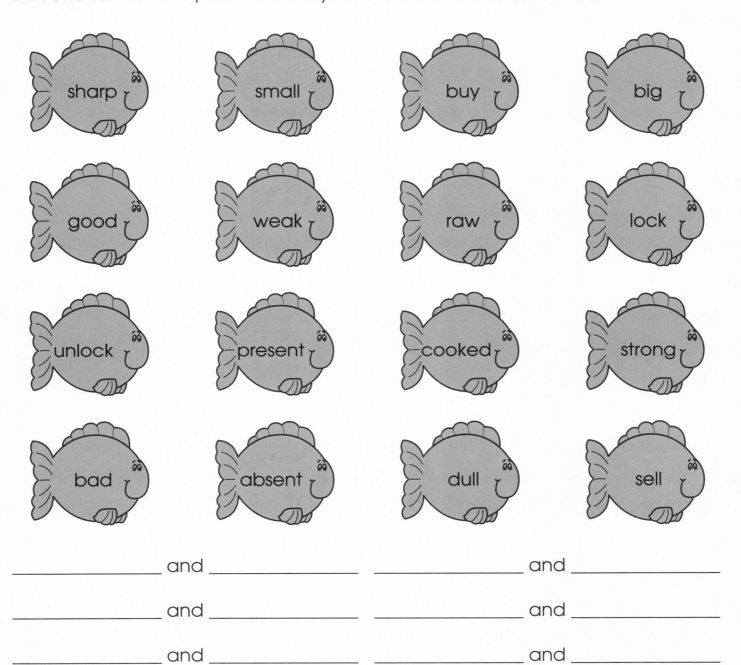

_____ and _____   _____ and _____

_____ and _____   _____ and _____

_____ and _____   _____ and _____

_____ and _____   _____ and _____

Try This!

On another sheet of paper, write the word *dull* in large letters.
Then, cross out the word and draw pictures to illustrate the antonyms of *dull*.

Wacky Word Pairs

Directions: Answer each question with a pair of words that sound the same but have different meanings. The first one has been done for you.

1. What do you call a bald grizzly? _____a bare bear_____

2. What do you call a mare with a sore throat? _____

3. What do you call a sweet doe?_____

4. What do you call an evening with a man in shining armor?_____

5. What do you call a frail seven days? _____

6. What do you call a reasonable cost of a bus ride?_____

7. What do you call a great trick with things you walk on? _____

8. What does a small insect call his uncle's wife? _____

Try This!

On another sheet of paper, write each pair of homophones in a sentence.

Could It Happen?

Directions: Each sentence has a pair of homographs. Read the sentence and circle the correct answer.

1. Could a man with a bow bow?   yes   no

2. Could you present your friend with a present?   yes   no

3. Can a tear tear?   yes   no

4. Will a door close if you get too close?   yes   no

5. Would a doctor have wound a bandage around that wound?   yes   no

6. Could the wind wind your watch?   yes   no

7. Could lead lead the parade?   yes   no

8. Do live animals live in the wild?   yes   no

Underline the homographs above.
Then, write the meaning of each homograph on another sheet of paper.

Directions: Read each sentence. Then, circle the letter for the correct definition of the underlined word as it is used in the sentence.

blow	a. hit; b. breathe out hard	**box**	a. fight; b. container
buck	a. dollar (slang); b. male deer	**drum**	a. beat or pound; b. musical instrument
peer	a. one of the same age; b. look at closely	**sharp**	a. pointed; b. alert or observant

1. <u>Bucks</u> have large, strong antlers.　　　　　　　　a　　b

2. The buck's <u>sharp</u> eyes look out for danger.　　　　a　　b

3. When in danger, a buck will <u>drum</u> the ground.　　　a　　b

4. A buck will stand on its hind legs to <u>box</u>.　　　　　a　　b

5. A buck can deliver a hard <u>blow</u> with his antlers.　　a　　b

6. The young deer will <u>peer</u> over the tall grass.　　　　a　　b

Try This!

Create a multiple-meaning wordbook. Use a dictionary if needed.

Bookworm Part 1

Directions: Use a highlighter to highlight each entry word and its part of speech. Then, use this dictionary page to answer the questions on page 28.

absorption–organic

absorption (*n*) 1. the process of being absorbed 2. entire mind taken over by something

clay (*n*) an earthy material that is made up of minerals and is often used to make brick and pottery

compost (*n*) a mixture used for fertilizing land (*v*) to convert to compost

decompose (*v*) 1. to break down into simpler compounds 2. rot

erosion (*n*) the process of eroding

gravel (*n*) 1. sand 2. loose pieces of rock

humidity (*n*) wetness in the air

inorganic (*adj*) 1. made up of something other than plants or animals 2. artificial

microbe (*n*) germ

mineral (*n*) 1. ore 2. something that is neither animal nor vegetable

organic (*adj*) 1. produced without using chemicals 2. natural

Try This!

Look up the above words in a dictionary.
On another sheet of paper, write the guide words for the page each word is on.

Bookworm Part 2

Directions: Answer the questions using the dictionary on page 27.

I. What is the quickest way to find out if the word *topsoil* will appear on this

dictionary page? _____

2. What do the abbreviations *n, v,* and *adj* stand for? _____

3. How many definitions are given for the word *decompose*?_____

4. Write a sentence with the word *organic*.

_____

5. Which word can be used as a noun or a verb? _____

6. What type of dictionary is this? How do you know?

_____

7. Write two more words that could be included on this dictionary page.

_____

8. Write two words that could not be included on this dictionary page.

_____

On another sheet of paper, compare and contrast a dictionary and a glossary.

Plants!

Directions: Cut out the flowerpots and glue them to the bottom of another sheet of paper. Add the correct punctuation to each sentence. Then, cut out and glue each sentence card above the correct flowerpot.

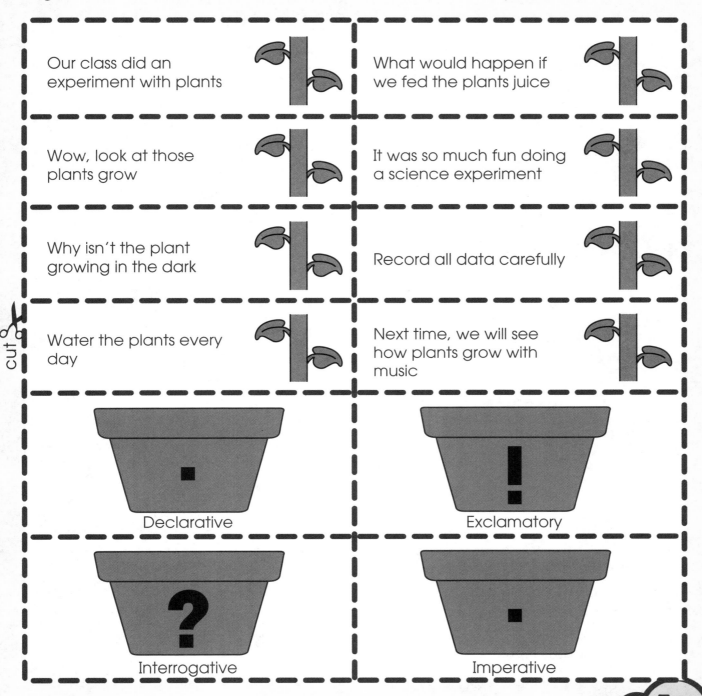

Our class did an experiment with plants

What would happen if we fed the plants juice

Wow, look at those plants grow

It was so much fun doing a science experiment

Why isn't the plant growing in the dark

Record all data carefully

Water the plants every day

Next time, we will see how plants grow with music

cut

Declarative

Exclamatory

Interrogative

Imperative

Try This!

Add two more sentences to each flowerpot.

To the Moon!

Directions: Combine each pair of sentences using *and, or, but,* or *so.* Write each compound sentence on the line.

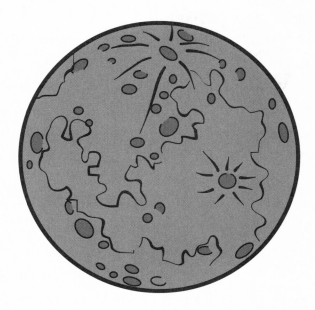

1. NASA built a spacecraft called *Apollo 11.* They launched it on July 16, 1969.

_____

2. Four days later, *Apollo 11* reached the moon. On July 20, Neil Armstrong and Buzz Aldrin walked on the moon.

_____

3. The astronauts took many pictures of the moon. They also collected 47 pounds of moon rocks.

_____

4. You can read about their moonwalk online. You can read about it in history books.

_____

Try This!

On another sheet of paper, write sentences using *and, or, but,* and *so.*

Subject Sleuth

Directions: Write the correct verb to complete each sentence.

1. In the summer, I _____ as a detective. (work, works)

2. I _____ neighborhood mysteries. (solve, solves)

3. When my friends _____ things, I help my friends find them. (lose, loses)

4. Jamie _____ things often. (lose, loses)

5. My friend Julio _____ me secret messages. (write, writes)

6. I _____ my decoder to figure them out. (use, uses)

7. I _____ my detective kit in a secret place. (keep, keeps)

8. Only my mom and dad _____ where it is. (know, knows)

On another sheet of paper, write an advertisement for a summer job you would like to have.

Star Code

Directions: Use the code to color the verbs.

present tense = yellow

past tense = orange

future tense = blue

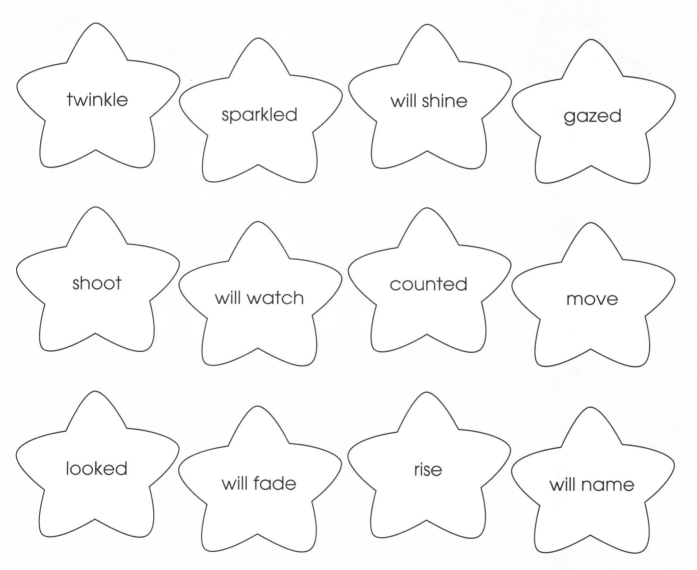

twinkle

sparkled

will shine

gazed

shoot

will watch

counted

move

looked

will fade

rise

will name

Try This!

Cut out the completed stars and glue them to another sheet of paper to form a constellation.

Growing Great Pronouns Part 1

Directions: Complete each cornstalk with nouns that could be replaced with the pronoun shown on the ear of corn.

Try This!

Find a paragraph in a book.
Replace each common and proper noun with the correct pronoun.

34

Growing Great Pronouns Part 2

Directions: Complete each cornstalk with nouns that could be replaced with the pronoun shown on the ear of corn.

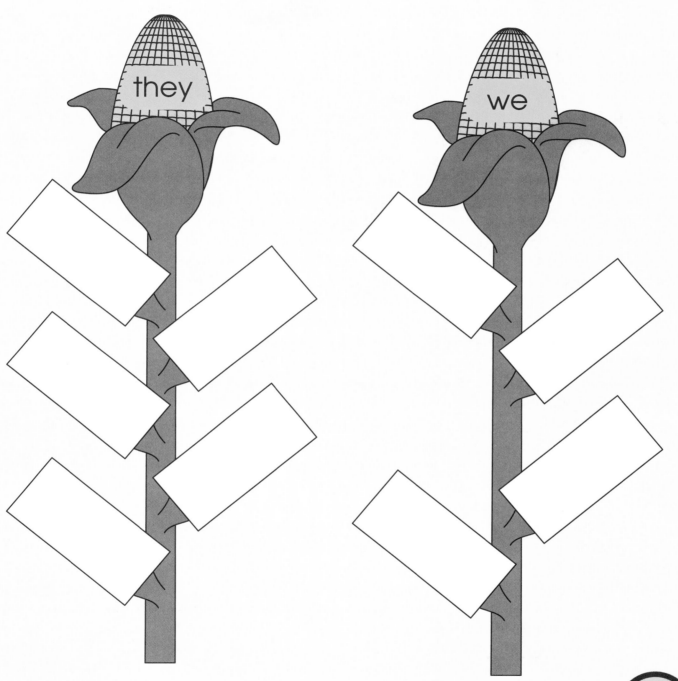

On another sheet of paper, write a story with a cornfield as the setting.
Use at least 10 pronouns in your story.

Once Upon a Time

Directions: Write three adjectives to describe each of the fairy-tale characters.

knight

_____

_____

_____

princess

_____

_____

_____

queen

_____

_____

_____

king

_____

_____

_____

giant

_____

_____

_____

prince

_____

_____

_____

Try This!

On another sheet of paper, write a fairy tale using some of the words above.

One Box, Two Boxes

Directions: Write the plural form of each noun.

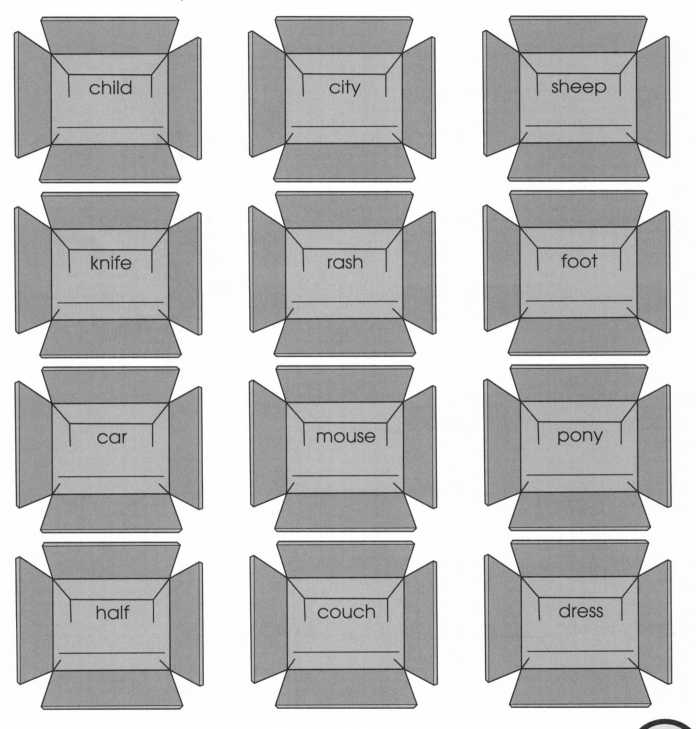

child

city

sheep

knife

rash

foot

car

mouse

pony

half

couch

dress

Try This!

On another sheet of paper, use each plural noun in a sentence.

It's Raining Apostrophes!

Directions: Use a different possessive noun to complete each sentence.

1. The three _____ paws were wet.

2. The _____ room was messy.

3. The _____ pencil was broken.

4. Both _____ grades were good.

5. That is _____ house across the street.

6. Some _____ uniforms were the wrong color.

7. We saw two _____ tracks along the path.

8. The _____ mailboxes were painted red.

On another sheet of paper, explain the difference between *dog's* and *dogs'*.

A Night on the Town

Directions: Write a proper noun for each common noun.

1. building _____

2. street _____

3. store _____

4. school _____

5. city _____

6. state _____

7. book _____

8. name _____

9. song _____

10. country _____

In a newspaper article, circle all of the common nouns and underline all of the proper nouns.

Happy Birthday to Me!

Directions: Complete the paragraph with information about your birthday. Cross out each letter that should be capitalized. Be sure to capitalize the words that you add if needed.

My Birthday

i love my birthday! my birthday is on _____.

i will be _____ years old on my next birthday. i was born on

_____ in _____. my family celebrates

my birthday with _____ .

I like to eat _____

on my birthday. On one of my birthdays, we went to _____ .

I had a great time!

On another sheet of paper, write about your best birthday. Provide a lot of details. Check your capitalization.

A Few of My Favorite Things

Directions: Provide at least three answers to each question in one complete sentence. Remember to use commas where they are needed.

1. What are some of your favorite foods?

_____

2. Who are some of your favorite friends?

_____

3. What are some of your favorite games?

_____

4. What are some of your favorite books?

_____

5. Where are some of your favorite places to go?

_____

6. What are some of your favorite toys?

_____

On another sheet of paper, write an essay about one of your favorites.
Use one of the answers above as your topic sentence.

Create a Country

Directions: Add the missing punctuation to each sentence.

1. Pilar created her own country

2. She created her country on October 29 2011

3. What would her country be like

4. What would be the law of the land

5. She wanted all citizens to be equal

6. Men women and children would have the same rights

7. All races religions and cultures would be respected

8. Everyone would live in peace

On another sheet of paper, describe a country that you would create.
What would be the most important laws?

Snack Time!

Directions: Cut out the names of the snacks below. Glue each name under the correct snack.

1.

Just thaw and serve!
What a treat!

2.

Fun to blow!
No sugar!

3.

Just add water,
mix, and heat!

4.

Fruity delicious!
Goes anywhere!

5.

Contains milk
and chocolate.
Nothing artificial added.

6.

Made with natural oats!
Goes anywhere!

| Juicy Frozen Fruit | All-Natural Ice Cream | Sugar-Free Bubble Gum |
| Instant Oatmeal | Fruit Bar | Granola Bar |

cut

Try This!

On another sheet of paper, write an advertisement for one of the packages shown.
Illustrate your advertisement.

How Seeds Spread

Directions: Cut out the topic sentences and glue them on another sheet of paper. Then, cut out the detail sentences and glue them under the correct topic sentence. Glue the labels to identify the topic sentences and the detail sentences.

Topic Sentences

Detail Sentences

Some seeds with spikes attach to animals' fur.	Dandelion seeds have parachutes.
Some sticky seeds attach to the feet of some animals.	Maple seeds have wings.
Animals eat seeds and move them to other locations through their waste.	The wind picks up some seeds and carries them.
The wind spreads seeds.	Animals spread seeds.

cut

On another sheet of paper, rewrite each topic sentence and its supporting details in a paragraph.

The History of Money

Directions: Cut out the sentences. Glue them in the correct order on another sheet of paper.

Then, Alexis and Emma went to the local library.

Alexis and Emma decided to research the history of money.

After the report was written, Alexis and Emma made a display.

Alexis read the book and then told Emma all about it.

Finally, the girls presented their report to the class.

Alexis and Emma's teacher gave them a research project.

Emma wrote the information in a report.

First, they looked online for important information.

There, they checked out a book called *The History of Money*.

cut

Try This!

Draw a cartoon about saving money. Your cartoon should illustrate each step in the correct order, such as earning money and putting money in a bank.

Pancake Breakfast

Directions: Read the recipe. Number the steps in the correct order.

Pancakes

Ingredients:

$\frac{3}{4}$ cup flour

1 tablespoon sugar

1 tablespoon baking powder

$\frac{1}{4}$ teaspoon salt

1 tablespoon melted butter

1 egg

$\frac{3}{4}$ cup milk

Steps:

_____ Cook the pancakes until they are lightly browned on both sides.

_____ In a small bowl, mix together melted butter, egg, and milk.

_____ Have an adult help you spoon $\frac{1}{4}$ cup of the pancake batter onto a heated skillet.

_____ In a large bowl, mix together flour, sugar, baking powder, and salt. Set aside.

_____ When bubbles start to appear in the pancake, flip it over with a spatula.

_____ Serve the pancakes with your favorite pancake topping and enjoy.

_____ Add the egg mixture to the flour mixture. Stir until it is well blended.

On another sheet of paper, write a recipe for one of your favorite treats.
Be sure to put the steps in the correct order.

Directions: Read the story. Then, write what happened next.

The children were playing baseball in the empty lot. Mischa was at bat. She swung hard and hit the ball farther than anyone else had. The ball sailed across the lot and smashed through Mrs. Avery's window. Mischa knew Mrs. Avery would be really angry. The other kids scattered. Mischa stood looking at the broken window.

_____

_____

_____

_____

_____

_____

_____

On another sheet of paper, write about what you would have done if you were Mischa.

What a View!

Directions: Use context clues to help you complete the passage using the words in the word bank.

astronauts	quickly	oceans
distance	data	world

Traveling in a space shuttle is fun. The _____ can see Earth from a distance of 160 miles. Because the space shuttle orbits Earth so _____, they also see several sunrises and sunsets in one day.

They pass over continents and _____. It is very easy to see the United States and the Pacific Ocean from that _____.

The space shuttle travels around the whole _____. It takes pictures and records _____ to bring back to NASA. The journey is incredible.

On another sheet of paper, draw a cartoon to illustrate each event in the passage above.

Complete the Story

Directions: Ask a friend to complete the story by filling in the blanks. Then, have your friend read the story to you, having you fill in the blanks. Count how many blanks you filled in the same as your friend.

 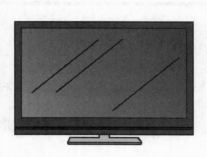 

For the Love of Movies

Hannah loved movies. She would stay up until _____ to watch
(time)

them. Her favorite characters were _____ _____ and
(describing word)   (type of person)

_____ _____. One night, Hannah stayed up really late.
(describing word)   (type of person)

The next morning, when she looked into a mirror, she saw a _____
(describing word)

_____. Hannah had turned into a character in a movie. Beware!
(type of person)

Don't stay up late watching movies, or who knows what may happen!

Fill in the blanks of the story again.
See if a friend can guess your responses.

What's Happening?

Directions: Read the story. Then, answer the questions.

Jack was uncomfortable. His new shirt was too stiff, and his tie felt tight. Mother had fussed over his hair, trying to get it to look just right. Finally, his mom smiled and said that Jack looked very handsome. Jack frowned. He didn't care about looking handsome.

Jack sat on the stool as he was told. He looked straight at the man his mother had hired. He didn't feel like smiling, but he did his best.

"Perfect!" said the man. "Let me get two more." Jack smiled two more times.

"That's it," said the man, "You're all done." The first thing Jack did was take off his tie!

1. What was Jack doing? _____

2. How does Jack feel about this event?_____

3. Who was the man who said, "Perfect!"? _____

4. Why did Jack take off his tie? _____

On another sheet of paper, write about what you think will happen next in the story.

53

Field Trip!

Directions: Read the story. Then, complete the organizer.

Jeremy's class was going on a field trip to the beach. They were going to see the tide pools. They were going to study the plants and the animals that lived there.

Jeremy had just moved to Los Angeles from Colorado. He had seen snow, bears, and mountains, but he had never seen the ocean. He was very excited.

The morning of the field trip, Jeremy could not get out of bed. His throat was really sore. Every time he tried to stand up, the room spun around. His mother came in to see if he was ready. When she saw him still in bed, she knew something must be wrong. She felt his forehead. He was running a fever.

"I'm not going to see the beach today, am I?" Jeremy asked.

"Not today. But, don't worry. The ocean will be there when you feel better. We will go then," his mother said.

Setting	Theme	Character

On another sheet of paper, make an organizer like the one above.
Then, fill out the organizer to tell about a time you went on a field trip.

54

Feature Hunt

Directions: Choose either your science or social studies textbook. Find an example of each text feature in the book. Then, write the page number where each feature is located.

Text Feature	Page Number
table of contents	
index	
glossary	
diagram	
photograph	
chart	
vocabulary word	

Make a bookmark that reminds you to check text features every time you read.

Waterworks

Directions: Read the diagram. Number the steps, in order, to show how water is purified.

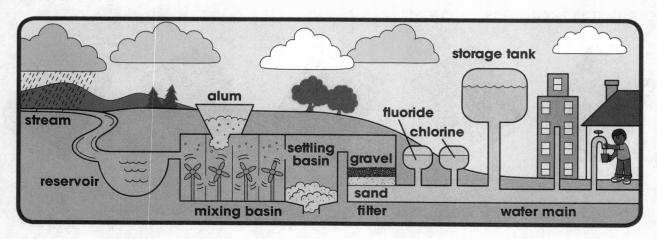

_____ The alum and dirt sink to the bottom of the settling basin.

_____ From the reservoir, water goes into a mixing basin.

_____ The clean water is stored in a large storage tank.

_____ First, raindrops fall into streams, lakes, and rivers.

_____ Water leaves the storage tank through water mains and reaches your home through your faucets.

_____ Alum is added to take the dirt out of the water.

_____ Fluoride and chlorine are added to the water.

_____ Then, the streams and rivers flow into a reservoir.

On another sheet of paper, write the definition of *chlorine*. Use a dictionary to help you if needed. Then, make a prediction as to why chlorine is added to water.

Flower City

Directions: Read the map. Then, answer the questions.

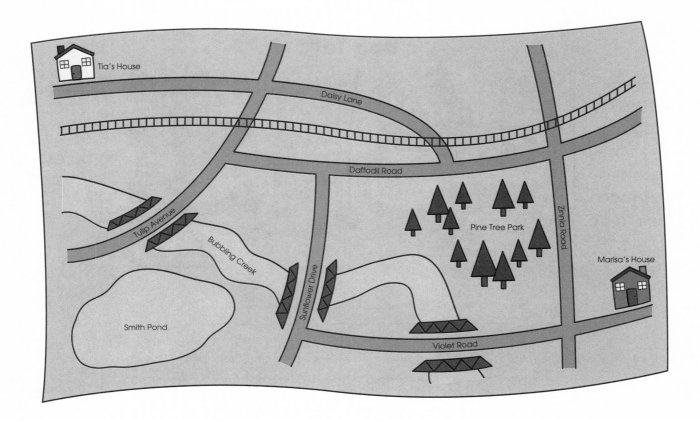

1. What three roads cross the railroad tracks? _____

2. What roads intersect both Daffodil Road and Violet Road? _____

3. How can you get across Bubbling Creek? _____

4. Give directions to get from Tia's house to Marisa's house. _____

_____

On another sheet of paper, draw and color a map of your neighborhood or an imaginary neighborhood.

Ready, Set, Draw!

Directions: Read each passage. Then, write if the passage was written to *inform*, *persuade*, or *entertain*.

Dog Tails

_____

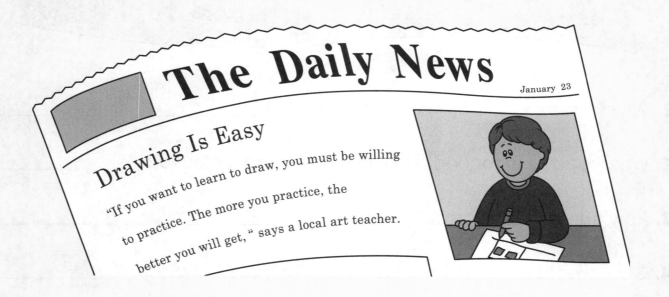

The Daily News

January 23

Drawing Is Easy

"If you want to learn to draw, you must be willing to practice. The more you practice, the better you will get," says a local art teacher.

_____

Try This!

On another sheet of paper, write a newspaper article that is meant to entertain.

Chirp! Chirp! Chirp!

Directions: Read each paragraph. Then, write one sentence to summarize the paragraph.

1. The baby birds were growing so quickly. Soon they would be flying. They were always hungry, so their mother flew back and forth all day long with worms and bugs for them to eat.

   _____

2. Chirpy was the smallest of the three babies. He was also the bravest. He liked to jump to the edge of the nest to see his new world. The mother bird warned him to be careful. She said that he might fall from the nest.

   _____

3. The mother bird flew away to get the babies their dinner. Chirpy hopped right up to the edge of the nest. Suddenly, his foot slipped. He began to fall. Luckily, the mother bird was there to nudge him safely back into the nest.

   _____

On another sheet of paper, rewrite this story from Chirpy's point of view.

Pretty Swans

Directions: Read each sentence. Write **X** in the **O** column if the sentence is an opinion. Write **X** in the **F** column if the sentence is a fact.

	O	F
1. Long ago, huge flocks of swans lived in America.		
2. Everyone loved these beautiful birds.		
3. These swans had white feathers.		
4. Swan feathers were used for writing with ink.		
5. Swan feathers were better for drawing than metal pens.		
6. A male swan is called a *cob*, and a female swan is called a *pen*.		
7. The sound a swan makes is hard on the ears.		
8. A refuge was started to protect the swans.		
9. It is wonderful to have a safe place for swans.		
10. Swans should be our national bird.		

Try This!

On another sheet of paper, draw a poster that will encourage people to save swans.

Who Said It?

Directions: Read each statement. If it is a fact, then Felipe said it. If it is an opinion, then Olivia said it. Circle the name of the person who said each statement.

1. "Eighth graders are too old to watch cartoons," complained Felipe/Olivia.

2. "A town square is part of a town," stated Felipe/Olivia.

3. "Enough rain can fall in one night to become a foot deep," explained Felipe/Olivia.

4. "Mr. Walker sells the best candy in the world," declared Felipe/Olivia.

5. "A dog is the best pet," said Felipe/Olivia.

6. "Winter is the season after autumn and before spring," stated Felipe/Olivia.

7. "Everyone likes to play in the snow," giggled Felipe/Olivia.

8. "Butter will melt on a hot pan," explained Felipe/Olivia.

Look at the ads in a magazine or a newspaper. Do they have mostly facts, opinions, or a mix of both? On another sheet of paper, explain why you think this is so.

School Day Drama

Directions: Draw a line to connect each cause and effect.

1. Our class won the contest,

2. After our class read *Charlotte's Web*,

3. School was let out early

4. Because Jan studied hard,

5. It was raining outside,

6. Chang's alarm did not go off,

7. Our class was excited

8. Because everyone followed the rules,

A. we learned about real spiders.

B. so recess was in the gym.

C. because we were going on a field trip.

D. so we got pizza at lunch.

E. she did well on her test.

F. because of the holiday.

G. so he was late for school.

H. no one got in trouble.

 **Try This!**

On another sheet of paper, make a list of other causes and effects you see at school.

Backyard Fun

Directions: Read each sentence. Decide if the underlined portion is the cause or the effect. Color the correct answer to reveal the path to the barbeque.

1. <u>Because it was a sunny day</u>, my family had a barbeque. (cause) (effect)

2. The food smelled good, <u>so the neighbors came over, too</u>. (cause) (effect)

3. Once the burgers finished cooking, <u>my dad put cheese on top of them</u>. (cause) (effect)

4. <u>My brother tripped</u> and spilled his food on the ground. (cause) (effect)

5. Because my brother spilled his food, <u>I couldn't stop laughing</u>. (cause) (effect)

6. Everyone was smiling <u>because we were having so much fun</u>! (cause) (effect)

7. The ants circled the picnic area <u>because they smelled food</u>. (cause) (effect)

8. Because the sun was going down, <u>we began to light candles</u>. (cause) (effect)

9. All of the kids were playing flashlight tag, <u>so the adults decided to play, too</u>. (cause) (effect)

10. <u>Because I had so much fun</u>, I will never forget that barbeque. (cause) (effect)

Try This!

On another sheet of paper, write five more cause-and-effect sentences about the barbeque.

Roller Coaster Rules

Directions: Follow the directions.

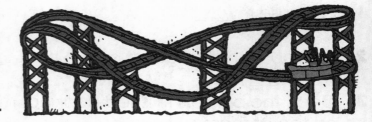

1. Color all two-syllable words blue.

2. Color all three-syllable words red.

3. Color all four-syllable words green.

4. Draw a yellow box around the words that start with the letter c.

5. Draw an orange **X** above the words that end with the letter e.

6. Draw a purple line above the words that have more than one a.

7. Circle all of the compound words in black.

8. Draw a pink **X** after the roller coaster name that you like best.

Millennium	Corkscrew	Lightning	Thunderbolt	Anaconda
Copperhead	Avalanche	Mountain	Thrill	Flashback
Speedy	Hair-Raiser	Splash	Twisted	Backlash

Create 10 more cards with a funny roller coaster name on each.
Follow the directions above.

Our United States

Directions: Follow the directions.

1. Write the abbreviation for your state on the state.

2. If a state is north of your state, color it blue.

3. If a state is south of your state, color it green.

4. If a state is east of your state, color it red.

5. If a state is west of your state, color it yellow.

6. Draw an **X** where four states meet at the same corner. (Hint: Four Corners in the West.)

7. Circle the two states that do not share a border with any other states.

8. Draw a star on a state that you would like to visit someday.

Try This!

On another sheet of paper, describe the route you would take to get from your state to a state you would like to visit.

About Frogs and Toads Part 1

Directions: Read the passage from a science book and answer the questions. Then, read the poem about frogs on page 67.

Then, read the poem about frogs on page 67.

Chapter 5 Lesson 1

Frogs and Toads

Both frogs and toads are amphibians (am•**fib**•ee•uhns). Amphibians spend part of their lives as water animals and part as land animals. In the early stages of their lives, amphibians breathe through gills. When they become adults, they develop lungs. Most amphibians lay eggs near water. Both frogs and toads are born with tails that they later lose. Both have poison glands in their skin to protect them from their enemies.

Frogs and toads are different in several ways. Most toads are broader, darker, and flatter than frogs. Their skin is drier. Toads are usually covered with warts, while frogs have smooth skin. Most toads live on land, while most frogs prefer being in or near the water.

Frog
lives in or near water
smooth skin

Toad
darker
drier, bumpy skin
lives on land

1. Is this passage fiction or nonfiction? _____

2. What is the purpose of this passage? _____

Try This!

On another sheet of paper, draw a poster that shows how frogs and toads are alike and how they are different.

About Frogs and Toads Part 2

Directions: Read the poem. Then, compare this passage with the passage about frogs on page 66.

My Frog Frank

My frog Frank is the best.
He gets to stay in my room,
even at night when it is time to rest.

My frog can hop like a rabbit,
and he can swim like a duck.
But, he does have one strange habit.

My frog Frank likes to tell jokes
about fish, bears, dogs, and toads.
Yet he hardly ever croaks.

1. Is this passage fiction or nonfiction? _____

2. What is the purpose of this passage? _____

3. Which passage would you use to learn about frogs? _____

Find a book about frogs. On another sheet of paper, draw a triple Venn diagram to compare the book to these two passages about frogs.

Flying Mammals

Directions: Read the passage and answer the questions. Use a crayon to underline each answer in the text in the color stated.

Bats

   Bats are helpful animals. They are the only mammals that can fly. They are some of the best insect hunters. Bats use their mouths and ears to find mosquitoes, mayflies, and moths. They can eat more than a million insects in one night. They help control the insect population. Although most bats eat only insects, some eat fruit and the nectar of flowers. Bats also help flowers by spreading seeds.

   More than 900 different kinds of bats are in the world. Some bats are small, measuring only $\frac{1}{2}$ inch (1.27 cm) long. Some bats are big. They can measure more than 16 inches (40.6 cm) long.

1. (yellow) How are bats helpful? _____

2. (blue)   How many different kinds of bats are in the world? _____

3. (red)   What do bats eat? _____

4. (green)   How large can some bats get? _____

On a large sheet of paper, use a ruler to draw the size of the smallest bat and the size of the largest bat.

A Special Day

Directions: Read the story. Then, answer the questions by circling the answers in the text.

Last summer, Maria and Lucy won free tickets to a water park. At the park, they floated down the lazy river ride and jumped the waves in the wave pool. They even slid down the tallest waterslide in the park! The girls ate frosty snow cones and cheesy pizza. By the end of the day, they were wet and tired, but happy. It had been a great day at the water park!

1. Who is in the story? Circle your answer in red.

2. Where did they go? Circle your answer in blue.

3. What four things did they do there? Circle your answers in green.

4. When did they go? Circle your answer in purple.

5. Why did they get to go there? Circle your answer in brown.

On another sheet of paper, draw a map of the water park that Maria and Lucy went to. Use details from the story to help you.

A Writing Robot

Directions: Choose a topic that you want to write about and write it in the top box. Then, complete the organizer with details about the topic.

Topic

Detail

Detail

Detail

Try This!

Use the organizer to write about your favorite sport.
Then, write a paragraph about your favorite sport on another sheet of paper.

For Sale

Directions: Read the advertisements. Underline the supporting details. Cross out information that is not needed.

Skateboard for Sale

Black-and-white skateboard with royal blue wheels for sale. Like new. It was my favorite board ever. I need to sell it before I can buy in-line skates. Also comes with cool stickers. Cost is $8.00. Call 555-0123.

Bike for Sale

I am selling my favorite bike. I got it for my sixth birthday. The bike is red with white stripes. Looks like new. I took really good care of it. Comes with a light and a basket. Cost is $15.00 or best offer. Call 555-0123.

On another sheet of paper, rewrite the advertisements, including only the important details.

Can You Sense It?

Directions: Write a story about something that happened in the school cafeteria. Use the organizer to help you use your senses to add details.

What did you see?	What did you hear?	What did you smell?

What did you taste?	What did you feel?

On another sheet of paper, use your five senses to describe your bedroom.
Then, draw a picture of your room.

Fiction vs. Nonfiction

Directions: Cut out and glue each book cover under the correct label.

Nonfiction	vs.	Fiction

cut ✂

Try This!

On another sheet of paper, draw a Venn diagram that compares a fiction and a nonfiction book of your choice.

Real or Historical?

Directions: Read each description. Then, write either **realistic fiction** or **historical fiction** on the line.

1. Anna is a young girl traveling west with her family in a covered wagon. *Out West* is a book that tells about the many adventures she and her family have along the way.

_____

2. Andre and Melissa have been best friends since first grade. Can they still remain friends even after a new kid moves into the neighborhood? Read *Friends Forever?* to find out.

_____

3. *Lost* is a book about the first settlers of North Carolina. A group of people came to North Carolina and lived among the Native Americans. After several months, the whole colony disappeared.

_____

4. Kennedy Elementary School was a very fun place to be in the 1970s. Holly, Megan, and Keisha were good students. The three of them decided to start a new club at school called *The Peace Group*.

_____

Try This!

On another sheet of paper, draw a movie poster about your favorite historical fiction book.

What Did You Say?

Directions: Write some phrases that different people might say.

A phrase my teacher might say: _____

_____

A phrase my friend might say: _____

_____

A phrase my neighbor might say: _____

_____

A phrase a parent might say: _____

_____

A phrase an older brother might say: _____

_____

On another sheet of paper, make a list of phrases your best friend says.
Then, write a story in your friend's voice.

They Win!

Directions: Read each situation. Then, write a sentence that the person might say. Be sure to use quotation marks and correct punctuation.

1. Ava's team just won the championship soccer game.

_____

2. Ava's dad is proud of the way she played the game.

_____

3. Ava's brother is happy for his sister.

_____

4. Ava's best friend likes the trophy.

_____

5. Ava feels very happy.

_____

Try This!

On another sheet of paper, write a story about Ava winning the championship soccer game. Include some of the dialogue that you wrote above.

It's a Dog's Life

Directions: Write a story about the dog's day using transition words such as *first, then, next, after,* and *finally.*

_____

_____

_____

_____

_____

_____

_____

_____

On another sheet of paper, draw a picture of what was happening with the dog right before your story started. Then, draw a picture of what happens to the dog after your story ends.

Camping Fun

Directions: Read the paragraph. Find and correct the 18 errors.

Camping can be so much fun last weekend, me and my family went camping in a park near the mountins. We took lots of stuff because we weren't sure what we would need. Dad and I set up the tents, while Mom and my brother built a campfire and make lunch. After lunch, we went swimming in the lake. Later, we went fishing my dad cot five fish! He cleaned it and cooked them over the campfire for diner. They tasted grate! After dinner, we tosted marshmallows and tell scary storys. I wasn't really afraid. Finally, we crawled inside our tents to go to sleep. It was quite except for the crickets. The next morning, we got up and starts another day of fun. I love camping?

Try This!

Create a brochure for a campsite near the Grand Canyon.

A Great Year

Directions: Read the paragraph. Find and correct the 22 errors.

Last year was alot of fun. In january, we went skiing in denver Colorado.

In february, my class performed a play about the life of martin Luther king,

jr. I got to play the part of dr king. In the spring, my family spent a weak at

the beech. We seen two baby sharks swiming around the fishing pier! During

the summer, I visited my Grandparents in Texas. I visited the space center in

houston. Finally, in december, I had the best birthday ever! I got a puppy. I

named him wolf because he looks like a baby wolf. Last year was relly a lot of

fun. I hope next year will be even better!

On another sheet of paper, write about a favorite thing you did with your family
last year.

Take Your Pick

Directions: Circle one item in each list. Then, write a descriptive paragraph about the words you circled. Use another sheet of paper if needed.

List 1	List 2	List 3
hamster	running	at the zoo
leopard	hiding	in the bathtub
bear	stuck	under the car
parrot	sleeping	in your desk
cricket	talking	on TV

_____

_____

_____

_____

_____

_____

_____

_____

Draw a picture of your favorite after-school snack.
Write a descriptive paragraph about it on another sheet of paper.

The Princess to the Rescue

Directions: Read the beginning of the fairy tale. Then, write two different solutions to the problem.

The princess had come to save the prince who was trapped in a deep hole. The princess brought only a rope, a rock, and a bucket of sand.

Solution I	Solution 2

Write the fairy tale from the point of view of the princess or the prince.

A School Story

Directions: Cut out the cards below. Choose one **Who**, **What**, **When**, **Where**, and **Why** card and write a story using those details.

Who?	Who?	Who?
a third-grade teacher and the principal	five students	the librarian and a cafeteria worker

What?	What?	What?
notice strange things happening	are suddenly very happy	disappeared

When?	When?	Where?
before school	after school	in the hallways

Where?	Why?	Why?
in the classroom	no one knows	because it was Saturday

cut ✂

Write two more cards for *Who, What, When, Where,* and *Why*. Choose one card from each type. Write another story using the new cards.

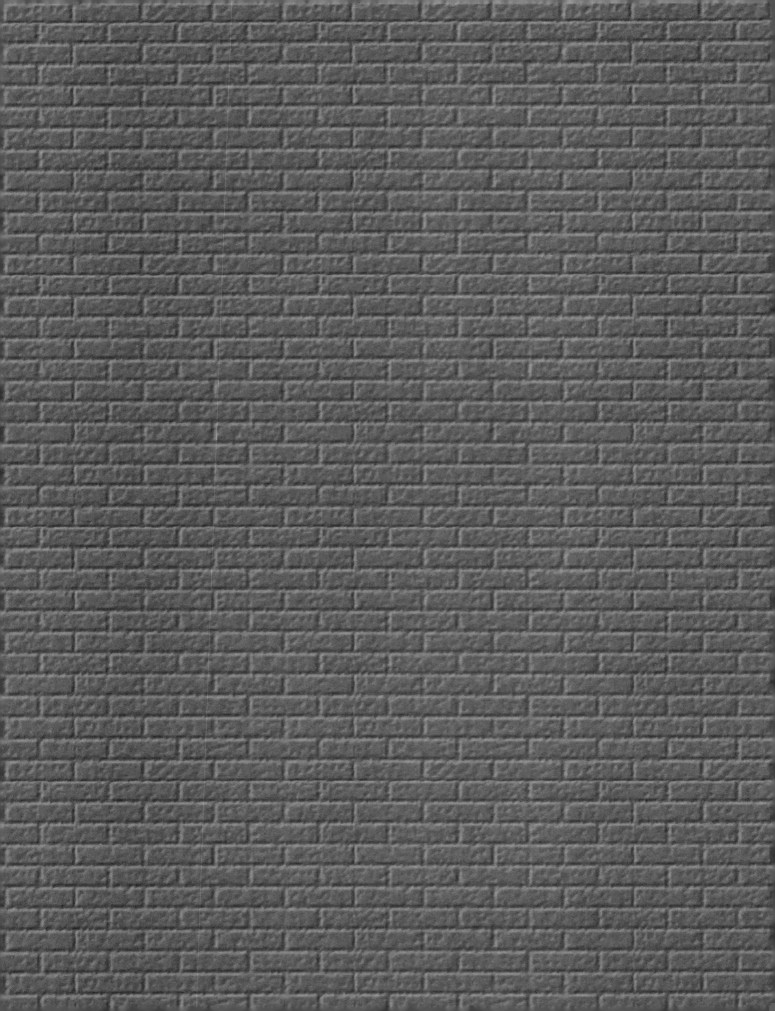

Problems Solved!

Directions: Choose one of the problems. Write an expository paragraph
explaining how you would solve the problem. Use another sheet of paper if
needed.

Problem 1	Problem 2	Problem 3
how to keep from being late	how to remember to bring necessary supplies to school	how to keep track of homework assignments

_____

_____

_____

_____

_____

_____

_____

_____

_____

**Many inventions were created out of a need to solve a problem. Draw a picture of an
invention you think might help solve one of the problems above.**

Frozen Yogurt Treat

Directions: Write an expository paragraph that explains how to make your favorite frozen yogurt treat.

_____

_____

_____

_____

_____

_____

_____

_____

On another sheet of paper, write a recipe for a cold treat.

Two Sides to Everything

Directions: Complete the organizer to respond to the question. Then, choose a side and write a persuasive paragraph on another sheet of paper.

Should students go to school year-round?

For	Against

On another sheet of paper, write a persuasive paragraph for the other side of the argument.

Laughable Limericks

Directions: Follow the pattern to write a limerick.

Limerick

A silly poem with five lines that tells a story.

The last words in lines 1, 2, and 5 rhyme.

The last words in lines 3 and 4 rhyme.

Example:

There once was a girl in third grade

who loved to sip lemonade.

She drank it all day

and then went to play

while drinking the 'ade she had made.

Try This!

On another sheet of paper, write another limerick and illustrate it.

Celebrating Cinquains

Directions: Follow the pattern to write a cinquain.

Cinquain

A poem with five lines shaped like a diamond

Line 1: a noun
Line 2: two adjectives describing the noun
Line 3: three *-ing* verbs describing the noun
Line 4: a phrase or a sentence about the noun
Line 5: a synonym for the noun

Example:
Big Dipper
beautiful, bright
shining, glittering, sparkling
home to the North Star
constellation

_____

_____

_____

_____

_____

Write a poem about the stars, the moon, or the sun.
Share it with a friend.

Answer Key

Page 6
1. Baker; 2. Barnaby; 3. Casper; 4. Dylan: 5. Harmon; 6. Jersey; 7. Laramie; 8. Leghorn; 9. Lester; 10. Newton.

Page 7
bl words: blink, blow, (blip); *fl* words: fly, flip, (flow); *cl* words: clasp, climb, (clip), (clink).

Page 8
1. sw; 2. st; 3. tw; 4. st; 5. sw; 6. tw.

Page 9
1. scout; 2. mountain; 3. trout; 4. flower; 5. shout; 6. shower; 7. tower; 8. count.

Page 10
Row 1: thumb, shirt, cheese; Row 2: shoe, thorn, check; Row 3: chin, shell, thermos.

Page 11
1. tent; 2. nest; 3. raft; 4. ant; 5. plant; 6. forest; 7. soft; 8. footprint.

Page 12
Row 1: couch, brush, mouth; Row 2: wreath, bath, dish; Row 3: bench, fish, cloth.

Page 13
grasshopper; skateboard; grandmother; bookshelf; popcorn; doghouse.

Page 15
Answers will vary.

Page 16
1. are not; 2. she will; 3. you are; 4. he is; 5. you will; 6. we are; 7. they are; 8. I am; 9. cannot.

Page 17
remake; unopened; unknown; unkind; distrust; rewrap; disrespect.

Page 19
–er words: teacher, worker, driver; *–ful* words: beautiful, doubtful, thoughtful; *–less* words: colorless, careless, meaningless.

Page 21
Across: 1. government; 3. harden; 4. washable; 5. development; 9. shipment; Down: 2. readable; 6. lighten; 7. enjoyable; 8. tighten.

Page 22

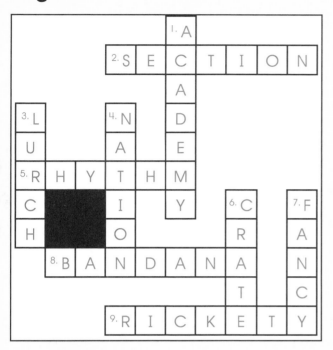

Page 23
unlock and lock; strong and weak; cooked and raw; bad and good; present and absent; sharp and dull; small and big; buy and sell.

Page 24
1. a bare bear; 2. a hoarse horse; 3. a dear deer; 4. a knight night; 5. a weak week; 6. a fair fare; 7. feet feat; 8. aunt ant.

Page 25
1. yes; 2. yes; 3. no; 4. no; 5. yes; 6. no; 7. no; 8. yes.

Page 26
1. b. male deer; 2. b. alert or observant; 3. a. beat or pound; 4. a. fight; 5. a. hit; 6. b. look at closely.

Page 27
absorption (*n*); clay (*n*); compost (*n*); decompose (*v*); erosion (*n*); gravel (*n*); humidity (*n*); inorganic (*adj*); microbe (*n*); mineral (*n*); organic (*adj*).

Page 28
1. Look at the guide words. 2. noun, verb, and adjective; 3. two; 4. Answers will vary. 5. compost; 6. science; Answers will vary. 7. Answers will vary. 8. Answers will vary.

Page 29
Our class did an experiment with plants. (declarative) Wow, look at those plants grow! (exclamatory) Why isn't the plant growing in the dark? (interrogative) Water the plants every day. (imperative) What would happen if we fed the plants juice? (interrogative) It was so much fun doing a science experiment! (exclamatory) Record all data carefully. (imperative) Next time, we will see how plants grow with music. (declarative).

Page 31
1. NASA built a spacecraft called *Apollo 11*, and they launched it

on July 16, 1969. 2. Four days later, *Apollo 11* reached the moon, and on July 20, Neil Armstrong and Buzz Aldrin walked on the moon. 3. The astronauts took many pictures of the moon, but they also collected 47 pounds of moon rocks. 4. You can read about their moonwalk online, or you can read about it in history books.

Page 32
1. work; 2. solve; 3. lose; 4. loses; 5. writes; 6. use; 7. keep; 8. know.

Page 33
present tense: twinkle, shoot, move, rise; past tense: sparkled, gazed, counted, looked; future tense: will shine, will watch, will fade, will name.

Page 34
Answers will vary.

Page 35
Answers will vary.

Page 36
Answers will vary.

Page 37
children; cities; sheep; knives; rashes; feet; cars; mice; ponies; halves; couches; dresses.

Page 38
Answers will vary.

Page 39
Answers will vary.

Page 40
Answers will vary.

Page 41
Answers will vary.

Page 42
1. Pilar created her own country. 2. She created her country on October 29, 2011. 3. What would her country be like? 4. What would be the law of the land? 5. She wanted all citizens to be equal. 6. Men, women, and children would have the same rights. 7. All races, religions, and cultures would be respected. 8. Everyone would live in peace.

Page 43
1. Juicy Frozen Fruit; 2. Sugar-Free Bubble Gum; 3. Instant Oatmeal; 4. Fruit Bar; 5. All-Natural Ice Cream; 6. Granola Bar.

Page 45
Topic sentence: The wind spreads seeds. Detail sentences: Dandelion seeds have parachutes. Maple seeds have wings. The wind picks up some seeds and carries them. Topic

sentence: Animals spread seeds. Detail sentences: Some seeds with spikes attach to animals' fur. Some sticky seeds attach to the feet of some animals. Animals eat seeds and move them to other locations through their waste.

Page 47

Alexis and Emma's teacher gave them a research project. Alexis and Emma decided to research the history of money. First, they looked online for important information. Then, Alexis and Emma went to the local library. There, they checked out a book called The History of Money. Alexis read the book and then told Emma all about it. Emma wrote the information in a report. After the report was written, Alexis and Emma made a display. Finally, the girls presented their report to the class.

Page 49

$\underline{6}$ Cook the pancakes until they are lightly browned on both sides.; $\underline{2}$ In a small bowl, mix together melted butter, egg, and milk.; $\underline{4}$ Have an adult help you spoon $\frac{1}{4}$ cup of the pancake batter on to a heated skillet.; $\underline{1}$ In a large bowl, mix together flour, sugar, baking powder, and salt. Set aside.; $\underline{5}$ When bubbles start to appear in the pancake, flip it over with a spatula.; $\underline{7}$ Serve the pancakes with your favorite pancake topping and enjoy.; $\underline{3}$ Add the egg mixture to the flour mixture. Stir until it is well blended.

Page 50

Answers will vary.

Page 51

Traveling in a space shuttle is fun. The <u>astronauts</u> can see Earth from a distance of 160 miles. Because the space shuttle orbits Earth so <u>quickly</u>, they also see several sunrises and sunsets in one day.

They pass over continents and <u>oceans</u>. It is very easy to see the United States and the Pacific Ocean from that <u>distance</u>.

The space shuttle travels around the whole <u>world</u>. It takes pictures and records <u>data</u> to bring back to NASA. The journey is incredible.

Page 52

Answers will vary.

Page 53

Answers will vary, but may include: 1. getting his picture taken; 2. unhappy; 3. photographer; 4. It was tight and uncomfortable.

Page 54
Setting: Los Angeles, CA, early morning, bedroom; Characters: Jeremy, Jeremy's mom; Theme: Jeremy has never been to the beach.

Page 55
Answers will vary.

Page 56
5 The alum and dirt sink to the bottom of the settling basin.; 3 From the reservoir, water goes into a mixing basin.; 7 The clean water is stored in a large storage tank.; 1 First, raindrops fall into streams, lakes, and rivers.; 8 Water leaves the storage tank through water mains and reaches your home through your faucets.; 4 Alum is added to take the dirt out of the water.; 6 Fluoride and chlorine are added to the water.; 2 Then, the streams and rivers flow into a reservoir.

Page 57
1. Daisy Lane, Tulip Avenue, Zinnia Road; 2. Zinnia Road and Sunflower Drive; 3. Tulip Avenue or Sunflower Drive; 4. Answers will vary but may include left on Daisy Lane, left on Daffodil Road, right on Zinnia Road, left on Violet Road, house is on left.

Page 58
Dog Tails: entertain; The Daily News: inform.

Page 59
Answers will vary but may include: 1. The baby birds, which were hungry and growing, were cared for by their mother. 2. Chirpy liked to jump near the edge of the nest. 3 Chirpy got too close to the edge one day and slipped, but his mother saved him.

Page 60
1. F; 2. O ; 3. F; 4. F; 5. O; 6. F; 7. O; 8. F; 9. O; 10. O.

Page 61
1. Olivia; 2. Felipe; 3. Felipe; 4. Olivia; 5. Olivia; 6. Felipe; 7. Olivia; 8. Felipe.

Page 62
1. D; 2. A; 3. F; 4. E; 5. B; 6. G; 7. C; 8. H.

Page 63
1. cause; 2. effect; 3. effect; 4. cause; 5. effect; 6. cause; 7. cause; 8. effect; 9. effect; 10. cause.

Page 64
Millennium: green; Corkscrew: blue, yellow box, circled; Lightning: blue; Thunderbolt: red, circled; Anaconda: green, purple line; Copperhead: red, yellow box, circled; Avalanche: red,

purple line, X; Mountain: blue; Thrill: nothing; Flashback: blue, purple line, circled; Speedy: blue; Hair-Raiser: red, purple line, circled; Splash: nothing; Twisted: blue; Backlash: blue, purple line, circled.

Page 65
Answers will vary.

Page 66
1. nonfiction; 2. to inform.

Page 67
1. fiction; 2. to entertain; 3. Frogs and Toads.

Page 68
1. Yellow: They are some of the best insect hunters. Bats help flowers and spread seeds. 2. Blue: More than 900 different kinds of bats; 3. Red: Although most bats eat only insects, some eat fruit and the nectar of flowers. 4. They can measure more than 16 inches (40.6 cm) long.

Page 69
Check that coloring and circling are correct. 1. Maria and Lucy; 2. the water park; 3. lazy river, wave pool, water slide, ate food; 4. last summer; 5. they won free tickets.

Page 70
Answers will vary.

Page 71
Skateboard for Sale
Black-and-white skateboard with royal blue wheels for sale. Like new. ~~It was my favorite board ever. I need to sell it before I can buy in-line skates.~~ Also comes with cool stickers. Cost is $8.00. Call 555-0123.
Bike for Sale
~~I am selling my favorite bike. I got it for my sixth birthday.~~ The bike is blue with white stripes. Looks like new. ~~I took really good care of it.~~ Comes with a light and a basket. Cost is $15.00 or best offer. Call 555-0123.

Page 72
Answers will vary.

Page 73
Penguins: Life in Antarctica (nonfiction); Perry Penguin: Private Investigator (fiction); Shake, Rattle, and Roll: Famous Earthquakes (nonfiction); Night of the Quakes (fiction); Moo! A Cow Joke Book (fiction); Moo! The Life of a Cow (nonfiction).

Page 75
1. historical fiction; 2. realistic fiction; 3. historical fiction; 4. realistic fiction.

Page 76
Answers will vary.

Page 77
Answers will vary.

Page 78
Answers will vary.

Page 79
Camping can be so much fun. **Last** weekend ~~me and~~ my family **and I** went camping in a park near the **mountains**. We took a lot of stuff because we weren't sure what we would need. Dad and I set up the tents, while Mom and my brother built a campfire and **made** lunch. After lunch, we went swimming in the lake. Later, we went fishing. **My** dad **caught** five fish! He cleaned **them** and cooked them over the campfire for **dinner**. They tasted **great**! After dinner, we **toasted** marshmallows and **told** scary **stories**. I wasn't really afraid. Finally, we crawled inside our tents to go to sleep. It was **quiet** except for the crickets. The next morning, we got up and **started** another day of fun. I love camping!

Page 80
Last year was **a lot** of fun. In **January**, we went skiing in **Denver**, Colorado. In **February**, my class performed a play about the life of **Martin** Luther King, **Jr.** I got to play the part of **Dr. King**. In the spring, my family spent a **week** at the **beach**. We **saw** two baby sharks **swimming** around the fishing pier! During the summer, I visited my **grandparents** in Texas. I visited the **Space Center** in **Houston**. Finally, in **December**, I had the best birthday ever! I got a puppy. I named him **Wolf** because he looks like a baby wolf. Last year was **really** a lot of fun. I hope next year will be even better!

Page 81
Answers will vary.

Page 82
Answers will vary.

Page 83
Answers will vary.

Page 85
Answers will vary.

Page 86
Answers will vary.

Page 87
Answers will vary.

Page 88
Answers will vary.

Page 89
Answers will vary.